Hot
strawberries

**Ron
Graves**

First published in Great Britain in 2016 by LEB Books,
a division of LEB Ltd, 57 Orrell Lane, Liverpool L9 8BX

© *Copyright 2016 Ron Graves*

ISBN 978-0-9934075-3-6

British Library Cataloguing in Publication Data.
A catalogue record for this book is available from the British Library.

The right of Ron Graves to be identified as the
author of this work has been asserted by him in accordance with the
Copyright, Design and Patent Act 1988.
Designed by Paul Etherington.

PICTURE CREDITS
Front Cover: Ron Graves
Rear Cover: Aimee Reid
Interior photographs: Marc A Price

dedication

For my parents and grandparents,
whose love laid the foundation for who I am.
And for my children, Cheyenne and Liam,
who are my favourite poems.

Ron Graves

about the author

Ron Graves grew up in Spennymoor, County Durham. He did not excel at school, but his English teachers noticed something positive about him and would often just let him choose what he wrote about.

After leaving school, aged fifteen, Ron worked in a hotel. Following an evening spent discussing the poetry of Gaius Valerius Catullus with a historian, Peter Farrier, who frequented the hotel bar and with whom he had become friends, Peter suggested Ron should get back to his education. His parents agreed and Ron spent the next seven years studying, before becoming a student psychiatric nurse, because he wanted to find out what happened in a big mental hospital ('the bin'). In total, Ron managed to remain a student for ten years.

Since 1982, he has worked as a psychotherapist with teenagers and thinks the energy and honesty of adolescents make them the best people to be around.

Due to the attraction of other pleasures, Ron's earlier poetic efforts were often put aside and forgotten about. Since he changed to only working as a therapist for a couple of days a week, however, he has discovered the joy of revising poetry. When he remembers where he put it.

introduction

Here is a collection of poems shaped around a life lived to the full, and a need to explain and illuminate and bear witness to that life; this writing communicates feelings and conveys ideas through rhythm, through the urgency of converting the spoken word to the page, through the care taken to be inclusive and not exclusive.

There is thought here, and it's the kind of deep thought that invites you in to swim around in it, not the kind of deep thought that drags you down like quicksand.

The poetry scene is in good, safe hands at the moment, and Ron's are a pair of the safest.

Enjoy the collection!

Ian McMillan
Poet and broadcaster
February 2016

acknowledgement

The author would like to thank everyone at A Pint of Poetry, Peterborough, for their encouragement and support since he first turned up to perform Jackie and the Chickens. (Well, Jackie was there, but the chickens weren't allowed in by the pub management due to some health and safety issues. As a result, he had to mime the fowls, which rather spoiled the overall effect. Even so, he was invited back and allowed to perform other poems on the strict understanding that neither wild nor domesticated creatures would be involved. So it was that, with one flick of a pub manager's tea towel, a lifetime's work was disqualified and poems such as Childe Harold's Ptarmigan, The Rime of the Ancient Marmoset and the much loved And Death Shall Have No Daddy Long Legs were lost forever.) He would also like to acknowledge his continuing collaboration in the field of song-writing with Mr David James Reid. Thanks, too, to Marc A Price for his wonderful photography. The author also acknowledges the work done in preparing this anthology by Paul Etherington at LEB Books.

contents

Hot strawberries

Ron
Graves

notebooks

i like shorthand notebooks
and the illusion they create
of order

        smooth white pages
            neat thin lines
           and the spiral
      holding everything together
             like dna

i like the little poems
that appear after i've forgotten
about the scratching i did
to spoil the calm order
of an untouched page

and i like the numbers
that put me in touch with
someone i thought was lost
but was only hiding
in the snowdrifts

celebrations

i cannot take my love away
to shows on trips for holidays

i cannot give her diamond rings
bracelets gowns and pretty things

i cannot reach for her at night
and draw her close as others might

i cannot wake but think of her
and all my sleep is dreams of her

the taste that's on my tongue is her
the scent brought by the breeze is her

the changing autumn trees are her:
the colour of her eyes

hot strawberries

1.

days were long then
and the time between christmases
stretched beyond the horizon
into a place where snow circled
slowly under street lamps
and ice ferns grew on the inside
of bedroom windowpanes

breath became frosty mist
like wispy dragons uncurling
from under the bedclothes
that you pulled tight around you
to keep out the cold
and you knew it was time to get up
when you heard mam raking ashes
in the fireplace but instead
you covered your head
with the soft sheet and heavy blankets
and pretended it was the middle of the night

i always had them pulled
around my head like a monk's cowl
to ward off the scary things
i knew liked to prowl
through the night time
and mam and dad unwound me as i slept
fearful i might suffocate
but in the inbetween time
there were sticklebacks to catch
and newts to net down at the reservoir
grasshoppers to put in a big sweet jar

holes punctured through the lid
so they could breath
tiny frogs to find in the uncut grass
that grew around the railing posts
at the brewery field football ground
mountainous slag heaps to climb
and career back down
on sheets of corrugated metal
mysteries concerning every kind of crime
from who slashed harry the wolf's show leeks
to what it actually was
that christine and mandy did
to keep them in the news of the world for weeks

my friend keith didn't know
but he wrapped himself in his mothers curtains
and danced on the coalhouse roof
in the hope of gaining some insight
that would lead him to the truth
he would be christine and i
someone called john
and that was it
just sitting in the living room
silent until we dissolved into laughter

and there were the rabbits and goats and pigeons
that lived in a place called the gardens
with chickens that sometimes
needed their throats cutting
whether they knew it or not
then there were the flowers
rows of scented flowers
as small as lily of the valley

as tall and full as chrysanthemums
waiting to be married to sprays of gypsophila
or hung on a wall like statis
until they became an everlasting
but dessicated beauty
and at the door of his cree
the shed from where he planned each step
in the design of this small eden
stood granda with a woodbine in his mouth

he had lost his right forearm
to the internal logic of a steam road-roller
when his shirt sleeve dangled
once too often and too low
over the uncovered mechanism
and the country boy's hand was dragged
down into the teeth of industry

after that he gave up road rolling
and became a renaissance man
cobbled shoes
raised chickens
bred canaries
slaughtered highland beasts
(a local butcher told me)
smithed iron
(the last smith in town said he was the best)
and dug a well at his allotment
that he fretted over for the rest of his life
cos a bairn might fall in
he told his wife
everywhere i went i heard about his talents
and my mother called him wonderful

once he found me crawling in the gap
between a new load of coal and the coalhouse roof
imitating my dad and the other heroes of the dark place
and afraid i'd get hurt
he told me to come out
and into the house
but i skulked outside and sat on the coalhouse roof
till grandma came home

she said i was afraid of him
and it hurt him to think it might be true
that a child was too scared to share his company
but i was just in awe of him and all he knew
about the world of plants and animals
and how with one hand he could bend it to his will
while others with all their limbs intact
just sat on the back step
watching an inattentive world drift by

he tried to teach me things
he thought would make life rich
true things about the beauty in everything
and the way everything depended on everything else
and he taught me to walk
by tying a long scarf around my waist
and helping me totter along the earth path
at the back of bessemer terrace
he helped me conquer gravity

i was the first grandchild
encouraged and tolerated in everything i did
and i would transform the kitchen
which was the daily living space

while the front room was only used for landmarks
like marriage birth and death
into red indian encampments
underground caverns
and magical places where everything was possible

the furniture was a mountain range
and i would scale chairs a table
a dresser pushed against the wall
under the guardian eye of my silent granda
who never once forbade my explorations
but sometimes lowered his newspaper
to signal that i should be careful
and i never tumbled
never fell
just learned that when descending
it is best to do it well

2.

i was almost ten when we moved out
of the mansion in clyde terrace
really only a two bedroom house
but to the little boy i was leaving behind
a cavernous place of mysterious staircases
and under the stairs a time machine
that looked like an ordinary cupboard
stripping away decades of wallpaper
my dad found a scrap of newsprint
that reported the defeat of custer
at the little big horn
and said savages outnumbered his cavalry
but i said i knew it was the sioux

the cheyenne and the arapahoe
who had bravely brought the invader to heel
and dad laughed about how i thought too much

i thought about the staircase
that went from behind a door
off the upstairs bathroom corridor
and up into a dark room where the attic should have been
sometimes i went through the door
climbed half a dozen stairs and lay there
wondering what was at the top
without ever having the nerve to find out

the day we moved
our things were loaded onto a cart
drawn by a horse too old for the job
that sullenly strolled down the road
with me and the owner singing behind
untroubled by the clatter of the radiogram
that never made another sound
after it hit the black tarmac

mam told me to keep the door shut
so the dog wouldn't get into the street
frantic with midday traffic
but i opened the door and out she ran
into a river of iron death
granda nursed her in the wash house
and mam turned on the radio
loud in the kitchen
so i wouldn't hear her dying howls

another day my ballerina cousin irene
had almost died saving me from
an oil tanker i'd excitedly stepped
in front of on our way to the circus
and catching me like an acrobat
she dragged me from under the wheel
and took the headlamp full in her face
and i sat with dad outside the emergency room
as a doctor came out mounted a stool
and turned up the music tannoy
so i couldn't hear her screams

irene got better after months in bed
and granda sent flowers every week
with fresh vegetables and fruits
to sustain her and give thanks
for the rescue of his foolish grandson
but she never danced again
not ballet anyway and all she had left
of that was fading photographs

but granda continued to be the man
i looked up to with a tremble
one day i was sent to a local cobbler
whose shop had a single light bulb
shaded with a halved tin that maybe
once held beans or scotch broth
and an atmosphere thick with dust
drifting in sunlight that had fought its way
through the dirty windows

then just as the tinkle of the door bell stopped
he appeared sullen as the horse that lost the radiogram
and looked at the tied together shoes
soled and heeled please I said
but hardly seeing me he dropped the pair on the counter
tell your grandfather to do them hisself
he's a better cobbler than me
i'd seen the iron feet that granda kept
in the big shed where once he bred canaries
but didn't know they were the lasts
on which shoes were crafted and repaired
now i didn't know what to make of the cobbler
when suddenly he was back
gathering up the worn shoes and sighing
tell him they'll be done for friday
before disappearing through a plastic curtain

3.

it seemed grandfathers could do everything
my other granda proved the trend when a roof fall
during another dangerous shift at the pit
cut him down and left him bleeding through a mattress
into a bowl placed under the bed
while the doctor argued for cutting off his leg
and the leg stubbornly stayed

my dad cut coal for other men to haul
out of the fertile belly of the earth
sang torch songs made catapults for his son
played cowboys and indians and taught him cricket
took him to the pictures and parochial hall
to see agatha christie melodramas

and told him about the spennymoor settlement
where coalminers wrote plays and books and poetry
painted pictures fine as anyone
and strove to turn the world to their desire

and so i grew from child to teenager
believing that a man did all these things
was all these things
and worked to make his love
material for his family

then one day coming back from school
i saw the drawn curtains at bessemer terrace
and didn't call as usually i did
but went straight home to find mam alone
dad was at the other house
where granda had lain ill for weeks
his lungs consumed by something called tb
and i knew what the closed curtains meant

granda had talked about poaching as a boy
in the fields and woods of lincolnshire
and the time he shot his teacher with an air rifle
during an escapade of truanting
then he spoke with his war-dead brother
who he said was there with father and mother
and just before he coughed
and blood ran over his cheek
in resolution of all worldly worries
he said i'm going to the allotment
to get ronnie a cup of hot strawberries

on falling

when falling
it is important
to relax
become a lark's sigh
or an angel's whisper
not much heavier
than the air
you fall through

not wise to
tighten up
stiffening in order
to fight
against the fall

that way
limbs will shatter
ribs will break
bones will be
forced through tissue
into body cavities
eye sockets
brain matter

but to fall
surrendering
to gravity
light as a
sea fret

is to make
safe landing possible
as when falling
from grace
we are caught
in the embrace
of a mother's love
or a lover's kiss

at the swimming pool

the bald man
who used to enjoy his hair
and now tries to be glad
for his smooth head
watches a girl
slipping into the blue illusion
of the swimming pool
graceful as a lover's smile
agile with deceit

and he wonders
if this is how it goes
that every moment
must be enjoyed
endured encapsulated
by a willingness
to garner value
from whatever is

then with her sharpened arc
she breaks the surface
shakes her hair
and scatters diamonds
full of sunlight and oceans
over the flat blue
echo of the sky

plain women

i dream of plain women
made beautiful by moonlight
the ordinary transformed
in silver beams
i dream of cold evenings
turning cosy
in the warmth of love
everything the opposite
of what it seems

i dream of flat fens
made undulant by shadows
the featureless transformed
by spirals and cubes
i dream of your gaze
distracted by absence
returned to me
with a smile
instead of your
distant frown

i dream of vines
entwined in the satisfaction
of comfortable love
under the sun of your smile
i dream of more
becoming something new
               this becoming that
                   was becoming is
 and i dream of you

the girl

South Tyrol, July, 2014

the sun looks lonely
when she isn't there
she with birds and bees
and flowers and trees
coming from her hair

she is a long cool mountain stream
a sparkling brook of hopes and dreams
she is the vein of melted snow
carrying the news you need to know

the wind is silent
when she doesn't sing
she with poems and songs
and chiming gongs
making your heart ring

she is a long cool mountain stream
a sparkling brook of hopes and dreams
she is the vein of melted snow
carrying the news you need to know

if the sky is missing
don't be surprised
if there are no seasons
you haven't lost your reason
they're in her eyes

she is a long cool mountain stream
a sparkling brook of hopes and dreams
she is the vein of melted snow
carrying the news you need to know

blade

thirty six school children nature study in the park
he had to get them back before it got dark
he was responsible and the deputy head
and pretty soon he'd think he was going to be dead

he saw the long lorry start to shed its load
as it turned the corner at the end of the road
shining sheet metal coming out like a blade
he didn't know what to do only that he was afraid

he could have run for his life
gone home to his wife
had his tea in peace and quiet
and avoided the knife

but he ran to the children and pushed them aside
which is how it was he nearly died
when the heavy sheet metal shining silver and blue
hit him from the side and almost cut him in two

he could have run for his life
gone home to his wife
had his tea in peace and quiet
and avoided the knife

after that they said he was never the same
he spent every day rotting with regret and shame
he sunk deeper and deeper into clinical depression
unable to get relief even from the confession
that he'd let the children come to harm
and his guilt was a rage that nothing could calm

he could have run for his life
gone home to his wife
had his tea in peace and quiet
and avoided the knife

when i saw him on the psychiatric ward
he was old and confused and shouting for tabs
it seemed like cigarettes were all he had
sometimes he'd shout about the kids in the class
by then mams and dads husbands and wives
he didn't know he was the hero who saved their lives

he could have run for his life
gone home to his wife
had his tea in peace and quiet
and avoided the knife

deep dark tomb

my father laboured in a deep dark tomb
where lay the compressed history of forests
woods and copses long asleep

no birds played here among bright leaves
nor sunlight broke between the boughs
to scatter diamonds on the ground beneath

but there were men and beasts with iron jaws
that excavated history with lightening bolts
and thunder that was harbinger of grief

and when the mighty fallen were awakened
brought out unshackled from their ancient rest
their power fuelled lamps to guide a new belief

that man made history in his image
from his imagination and design
and bent the tides of being to his bidding
to glorify himself until the end of time

box of paints

there's a man with an easel and a box of paints
and he's trying to discover light
in the dark black bowels of the groaning earth
where day is always night

there's another with a notepad and a draining pen
who is writing down the thoughts he's had
about growing up and falling down and being alive
and all the things that drive you mad

someone else has got a poem that he wants to read
about love and death and happiness and pain
and those pretty little flowers that still break through
though they're growing by a stinking drain

and they're down at the spennymoor settlement
the pitmen poets and painters
the big broad handed sons of toil
and the only true creators

tea is being poured into enamelled mugs
for sharing out between the men
like cornish and chaplin and the nameless ones
on who everything depends

there's a man from the allotments who just called in
with onions and leeks to pass around
cos you have to feed the body as well as the soul
when you're an artist underground
and everybody's working and speaking thoughts
about how to keep ideas in the air
like those jugglers in the circus with their fiery clubs
who know action is better than prayer

and they're down at the spennymoor settlement
the pitmen poets and painters
the gentle hearted sons of toil
and the only true creators

they're down at the spennymoor settlement
down at the spennymoor settlement
they're down at the spennymoor settlement
drawing light from the deep dark hole

all he ever wanted

all he ever wanted was his own cree
not big but enough to let him close the door
and keep away from that incessant howl
called other people's opinions
with a book
              a cup of darjeeling
and the clamour of his own thoughts
instead of the drone of everyone else's

but instead he had a greenhouse
where opinions flourished
infusing the hot air
from a radio tuned to radio 5 live
with the stink of stale supposing

i just think
they always say
as if they'd ever thought at all
and that i just
was shorthand for the sum
of a lifetime's reflection
instead of the hole where
thinking might have been
and so when the batteries died
he left the radio alone
and instead began to listen
for the sound of plants
                      steadily growing
as if likely to express gratitude
for his care and attention
after four years

five months
two days
six hours
twenty-three minutes
and seventeen seconds
he heard a noise
not the predictable rustle of leaves
thoughtlessly settling
against one another
but the sound of a voice
being found for the first time

and when he looked
he saw the radio
covered in mossy dust
and still where he left it
all those silent seasons ago
now with sound emerging
leafy and tendrilled
with ribs running through it
like the veins of a cock
hungry for communion
and the voice grew
and took him
wrapped him in its own need
to communicate
                    to connect
before crushing his chest
in the inevitability
of a cardiac arrest

jackie and the chickens

jackie kept his chickens in a cree down the allotments
and he liked to get the eggs to make an omelette every day
he fed them all the best things and pampered them like children
but they pulled their beaky faces soon as jackie turned away

jackie didn't know that they viewed him with contempt
until one day he caught them in the act
of sneering at his largess and mocking all his kindness
those chickens hated jackie and now he knew it for a fact

jackie jackie jackie
those fowls they cut him deep
they mocked him in the dust
and at night he couldn't sleep

so jackie brought his chopper and though it caused him pain
he chopped their little heads off as he called each one by name
his blood lust knew no limits as he slaughtered and he murdered
every two faced little chicken and then made liver pate

jackie jackie jackie
though it broke his heart to do
he took revenge on the treacherous birds
as he hacked and chopped and slew
jackie jackie jackie
he didn't take no shit
he was disparaged by the ones he loved
but he soon got over it

oh yes
he soon got over it
he did
he soon got over it
with aplomb
he soon got over it

darling

1.

darling
i am looking through the round window
with the chipped white sill
at a rainbow slowly forming
under the watercolour sky
where yesterday red streamers
stretched to the horizon
and i am grown sick
of being tired
and having no company
of listening to my own voice
of eating stale marmalade
on the wrong kind of toast
of the creaking boards
that once assured me
of birds in the attic
stairs that used to comfort me
with the sound of your feet
of the merry ding-dong-singalonga-paperboy
who ripped the paper
in the too-tight letter box
and gave me something trivial
to rail against
of the groan of my mind
going over the same old bullshit
till it sounds like my own voice
of listening to my own voice
of being trivial with my own voice
of having no company
darling

just looking again at the sky
where a rainbow came and went
without me having time to track its transport
i realise i am only alone
because i lost myself in you
in the gathering storm of mystery
before you went out
and i left myself at home

this is a depth i cannot fathom:
i am with you in you
yet languish here alone

2.

darling
i am in love
with the way you say the word
conjunctivitis
all emphasis on the con
and none left for the itis

let me take a moment to explain

at first
loving you
was all sighs and body fluids
looks like the gaze you get from someone
who has forgotten their glasses
hands clamped tight as in a horror movie
scared to let go in case solitude returned
with his razor sharp hands

and then
coziness arrived
the differences were laughed away
even toilet seats left up
and toothpaste squeezed in the middle
seemed innocent expressions of individuality
rather than acts of emotional terrorism
it was bearable

later
i came to notice
how you torment the life
out of words
like saying brought when you mean bought
sarah instead of sara
and renaming a tropical island sierra lanka
as if claiming it for the u s of a

what had these words done to you
what had i done to you
touch the collar of your coat like that
just one more time i thought
and i swear you'll be lucky
to get away with your life

so now i am embracing
the differences between us
as evidence of our creativity
and the space we have kept
for loving one another
in spite of everything

but touch the collar of you coat like that
just one more time and
i swear
i swear
my resolve to keep on loving
will be sorely tried

3.

darling
i am envious
of those young men
in tight shirts
who are afraid of everything
yet look content
as they slide up to women
in bars at railway stations
where they quickly impress
with a casual ability to flirt
and the promise of an affluent life

i am greedy
for their hungry look
their swagger and their apparent ability
to slip without effort
from the apprentice's cradle
into the blue bedrooms of women

i am thirsty
for the warm wet hellos they get
and the quickly satisfying fucks
between rounds of drinks

i am lonely
for even a dismissive glance

i am lost

4.

darling
li'l darlin'
i'm not so lonely
in this place near a bridge
swung across a stream or brook or beck
whatever it is

and i know you aren't alone
in thinking i'm a fool
but loving you has always been
a chore for me a duty
not to satisfy your needs but
to fulfil responsibility

you didn't ask for anything
but i had to provide
my job to bring in the prosciutto
and holidays in taormina and salerno
where the sea is always
warm enough to swim

as if you even wanted that
did you want that
did you want me ever
i don't think i ever wanted me

by the sea
jumping scree
imprisoned or free
a pain in the arse
a jokeless farce
that's me

5.

darling
every day i wonder how it came to this
no lovely cup of chocolate on an autumn night
no gentle goodnight kiss

no smile of coy approval for my tasteless joke
or quiet hushing to preserve my dignity
no conspiracy of whispers about the gormless bloke
who flirted with you on the beach at whitby

no cuddles in our bed when friends have left
finally allowing us to be alone
to blend into an hour of warming sex
with sighs and hugs and gratifying moans

now all we have is memories of the past
mine not the same as yours in fact
so different i don't know if we both were there
as i sit growing weary in this weathered chair

the fire's out i'm getting old
and like this room our love is cold

6.

darling
it's over now
i don't know who laid you there
or smoothed your dress
and brushed your hair
i wouldn't even care
if only you had stayed

but now you've gone

your lover's call more irresistible
than my unspoken wish
so when he came for you
there was no effort to resist
you didn't even fight
but yielded soft
and disappeared in the night

organised

a baby with a broken neck
an uncle in an apron
some glasses tipped onto the floor
a bottle not yet empty

this is the order or our living
the way that things are organised

a bottle with a broken neck
an uncle not yet empty
a baby tossed onto the floor
some glasses and an apron

this is the order or our living
the way that things are organised

a baby with a bottle
some glasses and an apron
an empty uncle on the floor
a broken neck

this is the order or our living
this is the structure of our lives
the way that things have just turned out
the way that things are organised

leap

i am a man who cannot leap
scott free into receiving air
ready to accept his gift of despair
and carry him a while
because i am cursed with the burden of hope

and i know that four floors down
i'll be thinking about those girls
cruising the shopping mall
and guessing that maybe
life isn't too bad after all

then ten floors more
and it seems so far so good
as my confidence begins to grow
self–loathing replaced with a smile
of forbearing empathy
for the falling forever dope
faced with uncompromising concrete
hard as a reality test

and in a moment of joyous ignorance
i flap and pedal like an ostrich on a tricycle
then STOP suddenly
and spend the immensity of forever
in a state of disappointment

so instead
i hang on hoping
that the disappointment isn't really real
and that tomorrow
all my hopes will

quell my fears
maybe one of those girls
needs a shoulder to cry on
maybe one of those shoulders
needs a tear

factory

when the factory closes
bring your heart home
and i will sooth you
with rice and cinnamon
in a bowl of sweet milk

yours will be the golden skin
rich as sugared almonds
and the sweetness will protect you
against bitterness and spite
as you curl with me through the night

but tomorrow darling
you will go back
to the dull dreamtime
of the production line
where your heart counts for nothing
and your will is drained

do i give you
the strength to keep going
with my tenderness and warmth
or do i sweeten the poison
that chokes your soul
and makes waking death possible

black

everything is black
black with blood
black with night
black with death
black with the desire i felt
for the woman at the
supermarket
but can desire be black

or is it the concentrated light
of stars alive and dead
striving to express itself
in a burst of brilliance
between strangers for whom
there is no ulterior motive
just the need to shine

and is shining the flame
that burns through the obvious
futility of waking every day
for what would otherwise
be nothing more than
twelve hours of loneliness
before sleep takes us again

everything is black
black with the concentrated
experience of generations
striving against darkness
to make being bearable
everything is black
and why we desire

the girl I loved

the girl i loved when i was seven
had ginger in her hair
and freckled skin
her mouth was a small pink cupid bow
and her ears held her hair
like curtain rings

i did the clichés all for her
sighed moaned and dreamed and carried books

then once
just once
i dared that once
to kiss her on the cheek before we parted
she with her books back in her arms
and me on the brink of being broken hearted

johnnie ray

my mother had a photograph of johnnie ray
that he signed when unexpectedly one day
he turned up in a pub called the thinford inn
which my dad just happened to be drinking in

johnnie couldn't sing cos he had a gig that night
but everyone understood and said it was alright
then the landlady gave him her husband's dinner
and my dad was persuaded to be the singer

so johnnie ray played piano and cliff graves sang
and then they had a conversation man to man
when johnnie said 'you're a better singer than me'
and signed that photo writing 'love to deannie.'

my mother loved to hear johnnie ray
cos he cried when he sang and gave his feelings away
he was the nabob of sob he was mister emotion
and even broken hearted he maintained his devotion
to the little white cloud and walking in the rain
and he didn't even try to disguise his pain

tossed in a blanket till his hearing failed
the oregon boy had sobbed and wailed
because he wanted the music but he only had a fuzz
no clear sweet notes in that deafening buzz

so he sang his own songs to fill the gap
and he didn't just sing about the pain of that
he taught me to give my heart in sweet surrender
how well i remember i'll always remember

ooh that night ooh what a night it was
it really was such a night
came the dawn and my heart and my love
and the night were gone
but i'll never forget that kiss in the moonlight
such a kiss ooh such a night

my mother loved to hear johnnie ray
cos he ached when he sang and let his feelings sway
he was the nabob of sob he was mister emotion
and when it came to cry his tears were the ocean

autumn

when autumn tea times
wrap you in their charcoal arms
and quiet closes on the rowdy day
the smell of comfort rising
from the kitchen hearth
will you remember anything i say

while i am gathering
blackberries in a milk tin
and spiders weave new webs around my hands
each perfect pass
made with a surgeon's skill
i will be dreaming of a lover's plans

the night grows frosty
but our gathering in
combines us in a pact against the cold
i draw you closer
and you burrow down
our bodies wrapped in every curve and fold

when autumn tea times
wrap you in their charcoal arms
and quiet closes on the rowdy day
the smell of comfort rising
from the kitchen hearth
will you remember anything i say

love her less

i've been loving her more than anyone before
and now i'm in a terrible mess
so i'm looking for a way to call it a day
by learning how to love her less

but when i'm with her the sun comes up
and her voice makes the morning star shine
even though she's with another and it breaks my heart
deep down i think she'll always be mine

so i keep hanging in with a hope and a prayer
and tell myself things will be fine
cos i'm clinging to the hope that she feels like me
and deep down knows she's mine

i've been loving her more than anyone before
and now i'm i'm in a terrible mess
so i'm looking for a way to call it a day
by learning how to love her less

but i can't really do it and the plan is flawed
cos no one should deny the way they feel
and if i ever manage to love her less
i know it means i won't be real

so i try to put my feelings in a tidy little box
and lock it in the space under the stairs
where i hope the night time creatures might pick it up
and imagine the feelings are theirs

i've been loving her more than anyone before
and now i'm i'm in a terrible mess
so i'm looking for a way to call it a day
by learning how to love her less

love lost to the season

i broke the misery of every day
by standing in the strained light of the evermore
and saw her face glow in the summer sun
that lazily shone through leaves of sycamore

i held her in imagination
so close it seemed we grew as from one seed
entwined like vines around a weathered trellis
bearing sweet fruit our love would always feed

but autumn comes and passes into those
cold winter days that blind the sun
with bitter remonstrance against such youthful joy
as spring and summer playfully confer
upon the poet lover and the kissing pair

instead of reckless loving and abandoned skirts
winter demands security and buttoned shirts
and so our growing as a perfect one was stopped
and separateness that proves the fact of loss
replaced our easy happiness with yawns of dulling hurt

mornings

on mornings like this
when grey clouds close the sky
and she is somewhere far from me
with like clouds drifting in her eyes
i remember other cloudy days
and other women who would comfort me

my mother and grandmothers
an auntie hoisting me onto her knee
maria who hung out of a window
hinting at the beauty of her breasts
while on a working holiday from italy

and i drift with the clouds
but back in time to former days
when only crackling ice and melting snow
might complicate a day
and jess the dog would come for me
calling me back for sunday dinner
while i was dreaming time away

i did not know on those sweet solstice days
that loneliness and yearning come
when love has banished solitary ease
and needing her has brought me to my knees

am i?

first
      there was the pleasure of her company
and then the chaste goodnight kiss
followed by a message
and slight vertigo
            before i fell

down through half-recovered memories
and unsuppressed wishes
faster and faster with a thrill
like conception might be
for the fertilised egg
on a helter-skelter to embedding
some time after frolics
behind the door at a mafia wedding

but then
there were knocks and minor injuries
sustained when hitting branches
and rocky fingers hidden in the clouds
it hurt
      almost made me turn back
but falling does not allow returns
and so it went on until eventually
i thought i'd stopped
the vertigo spin
had certainly alleviated
but i had no bearings
          no point of reference
for my new location
and still i seemed to be above myself

half landed
         half in air
half joy
     half misery
half sure
      half completely unaware

what's happening?

is this being done to me?
am i doing this to myself?
did i really fall
         am i falling still?
am i mad
     or am i ill?

i think i was up there
but don't remember what's above
maybe i'm dreaming
         or maybe i'm drunk
maybe i'm lost
     or maybe i'm in love

buttercup

build me up buttercup
was the song all the girls were singing
tight in their ice blue denim jeans
shrunk during unnecessary bathing
on empty evenings

i was the kid
who liked watching
and imagining himself close
to those inviting looks and secret curves
that concealed something
something mysterious and out of the ordinary

like lamb chops with mint
on a sunday afternoon
fresh from the farm without
pain and misery
no cruelty in the hearts of these girls

just warm softness
and a taste for adventure
like kissing schoolboys
on rainy porches

the old fuck

the old fuck at the counter
with the frayed jeans full of water
where they sucked up the rain
can't decide whether he wants the money in tens or twenties
the guy behind me wants to punch him in the head
then the old fuck turns round
and says what's the matter with you
he's talking to me
so i thumb over my shoulder
and say he wants to know how long you'll be
and the old fuck says
as long as it fucken takes
that's life
so there you have it
from the mouth of the old fuck himself
it takes as long as it takes

bowline

she comes to me in the night
feathery as a zephyr
drawn to me by the light
of my nocturnal longing

and lays across me
like a sea creature hungry for love
all tentacles and suckers
searching for the nourishment
that satisfied desire yields

she comes to me in darkness
shifting through the silent air
to put me in a slippery harness
made of seaweed

then she rides me
through the spumy churning waves
and takes me down to where
there is no light
but magic creatures live

and when i wake she is not there
there is no watery mark
there is no point to search for she
who comes from in the dark

she will not stay she will not wait
i wish she'd keep me there
below the folding ocean tide
far from this choking air

it's a long day
at the
paper cup factory

('Well! A woman that can fart is not yet dead!' –
the dying words of La Contessa Therese Di Vercelis,
as reported by Jean-Jacques Rousseau)

it's a long day at the paper cup factory
somebody farts for light relief
and the iron grip of necessity seems to loosen
till the charge hand
                                 hungry for progress
calls everyone to attention
                                 and a pep talk starts

'this is a job where a person can advance
but you have to make an effort and
listen up
            keep your head down
                                 meet the targets
all this farting around will get you nowhere'

and the surreal tension
between the urgent task
of making paper cups
to put in cardboard boxes
to send to people in paper cup factories
to drink their pissy coffee from
while they're making paper cups
to put in cardboard boxes
to send to people in paper cup factories
to drink their pissy coffee from
and the rowdy expression
of bodily gasses
expelled in a deathly moment of hopelessness
either breaks your heart
                        or like la contessa di vercellis
tells you life goes on
so long as you can fart

friday woman

i loved her dirty beauty
and her tawdry kindliness
when she offered me the comfort
that she kept beneath her dress

i loved her warmth on winter mornings
in the crumpled nightwrecked bed
with a hand around her breast
and an arm beneath her head

i loved her drunk or softly sober
standing straight or bending over
lying down among the clover
like the old folk singer said

i loved her pretty thinking
and the way she'd always see
that the causes of my suffering
came directly from in me

i loved she never mentioned it
or tried to push the point
and wouldn't punch a poor man's nose
just to put it out of joint

but still there's how she handled me
trained me up and cut me free
showed me lovely things to see
then dumped me like i'm dead

i loved her dirty beauty
and her tawdry kindliness
when she offered me the comfort
that she kept beneath her dress

cream crackers

cream cracker biscuit tin economics
tells you that there's plenty for everyone
but a few get crisp and tasty biscuits
while there's only crumbs for the millions and one

maggie licks her fingers at the prospect of cheese
and mikey chooses honey while he worries about the bees
the kids have the choice of either of these
while asha and ahmed are working on their knees

cream cracker biscuit tin economics
tells you that the good stuff trickles down
a few get silver bracelets and fine perfume
while what trickles to the rest is stinky brown

gemma likes the feel of her nina ricci coat
and gordon knots a lacroix tie around his throat
the children get a castle with a fish-filled moat
while femi and furaha have to eat their goat

cream cracker biscuit tin economics
says everyone's equal if you've got the cash
if you haven't got money you can mortgage your house
and hope the fat cat banks don't crash

clarissa packs the twins off to boarding school
jeremy thinks his lexus looks really cool
their offspring are specialists in misrule
while chang and yin draw water from a fetid pool

cream cracker biscuit tin economics
says that there's plenty for everyone
but while a few get dreams fulfilled
it's a nightmare for the millions and one

almost seduction

i was almost seduced by a woman in uniform
her eyes were cold but her body was warm

she said she'd didn't really fancy me much
but was draw by my political conviction and such

she said she once knew a man who was a communist
and it always turned her on when he made a fist

so she called for me when she needed assistance
and though i tried to resist she was very persistent

then one evening when she asked me to change a plug
we both ended up on the front lounge rug

and i thought i was finally gonna get laid
by the woman who was the head chambermaid

but she said not here now don't make a fuss
and i said i had to catch my last bus

this is what can happen when you're just sixteen
and you don't understand things are as they seem

i was almost seduced by a woman in uniform
her eyes were cold but her body was warm

weight

sometimes i get heavy in the extremities

not the physical ones

they kind of make their own arrangements

but the ones that reach out from the heart

when that happens

i drop my guard and just about

everything else i'm trying to hold up

but usually

i look at you

or think of you

or reach for you

and there is nothing but

lightness and a sense of elevation

usually

your being

makes my being

the essence of being

and there is nothing but

the look that goes between us

sometimes i wonder where you are

not gone missing

and not only in physical reality

but where in relation to the grain called me

usually

i look for you

picture the sight of you

imagine the sound of you

breath in the heady scent of you

always

i find you

in everything

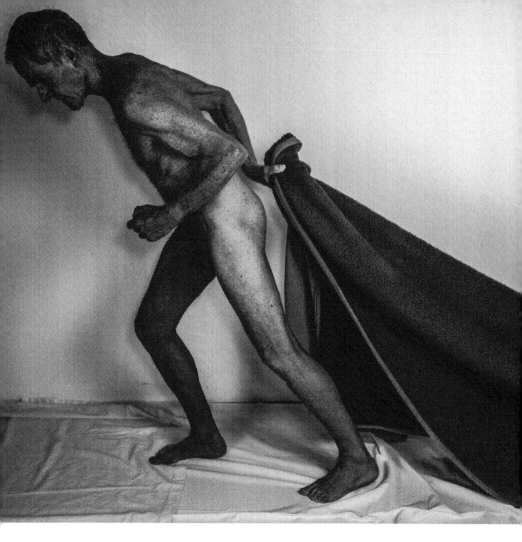

arses

when i wiped the arses of old men
sometimes in the thin light
from a squinting door
so not to waken the sleepers
quiet between crisp white sheets
and a green honeycomb blanket
topped with the regulation cream coverlet
i would think of the pleasant things
that waited for me when the shift ended

like a long drink in the hospital social club
and a slow fuck with a student nurse back in my room
and i would try to be patient
with the confused old man
who probably thought i was trying to rob him
or rape him or take what remained of his mind
full of mixed up memories of love and loss
and pigeons and pussycats
cabbages and cornflowers tall as cathedrals
weekends picking coal at blackhall rocks
used condoms among the dunes
fights in boxing booths during the recession
over married women bus drivers
and thoughts of disrespect from strangers
but when it came down to it
i was wiping shit off an old man's arse
and the only one who knew
what was happening was me
i could have left it for the night shift to find
dry and caked and stuck to his papery skin
and gone for that drink and that fuck
without the resistant odour of piss and shit
clinging to my hands like phosphorus
as a reminder that i was a wiper of old men's arses
but men and women not yet old
had wiped my arse and held my hand
taught me how to walk and
shown me how to be a man
how to laugh and cry and drink and fuck
and wipe the arses of old men like a man

so i wiped and washed and tucked the old man in
pulled the bedclothes round to keep him warm
said his name and wished him pleasant dreams
of love and loss and pigeons and pussycats
cabbages and cornflowers tall as cathedrals
weekends picking coal at blackhall rocks
and when in the early hours his life drifted out
he was warm and as clean as the day his mother bore him

curve of the earth

he saw the curve of the earth
in the shape of her breast
he heard the sound of the spheres
whisper in her voice
he felt the wisdom of a healer
in the touch of her hand
and he weighed all the odds
when he made his choice

he put the money in the packet
on the bedside chair
then he lay down on the bed
alongside her
he put the money in the packet
on the bedside chair
then he lay down on the bed
alongside her

he saw the curve of the earth
in the shape of her breast
he heard the sound of the spheres
whisper in her voice
he felt the wisdom of a healer
in the touch of her hand
and he weighed all the odds
when he made his choice
she stroked his tired brow
and she straightened his tie
she heard his heavy breathing
like a weary sigh
she stroked his tired brow
and she loosened his tie
she had no way to know
he was about to die

he saw the curve of the earth
in the shape of her breast
he heard the sound of the spheres
whisper in her voice
he felt the wisdom of a healer
in the touch of her hand
and he weighed all the odds
when he made his choice

from each

*A 2002 Columbia Law School Study reported that two thirds of
Americans thought this quote came from the US Constitution:
'From each according to their ability, to each according to their
need' (Karl Marx, Critique of the Gotha Program, 1875)*

i'd had an egg on toast
cos that's all there was to eat
and as i was walking to my work
i met him in the street

he said i've had breakfast fit for a king
a perfect start to the day
and then he made me listen
to all he had to say

i've had sausage and beans tomatoes and greens
both black and white pudding too
liver and bacon unless i'm mistaken
and left over irish stew

fourteen slices of toast and a weekend pot roast
with bread fried in the finest goose fat
sizzling hot in the pan to please a man
so what do you think of that

i said i've had an egg on toast
cos that's all there was to eat
yet still i stand upright
and walk on my own feet
whereas you i have noted
though declaiming full throated
are wheeled in a chair down the street
and he said

for lunch i'll have pheasant with roasted potatoes
chitlins and mushrooms in thick garlic sauce
three large bowls of soup to precede where the rest goes
washed down with two bottles of wine per course

high tea will be made of a light repast
of cress and cucumber white sandwiches
perhaps twenty of each with a good leg of meat
so as not to outstretch my britches

oh and beer and wine and a whisky or two
just to moisten the morsels i'm trying
for it never is wise to give dry food a try
while supper is gradually frying

i said i've had an egg on toast
cos that's all there was to eat
yet still i stand upright
and walk on my own feet
whereas you haven't answered the question implied
about how you can live or even survive
when your diet's so rich and of so much compiled
and he said

i've eaten buckets of fishes wheelbarrows of fowls
whole tribes of hooved beasties and cloven
i don't use knives and forks but shovels and trowels
and if there's one thing my diet has proven
it's this mighty frame which my mother bequeathed
from her own stately bosom and thighs
must be nourished by mountains of fresh meat not seeds
or the thin legs of spiders and flies

my appetite is such i could eat up the earth
with your children and babies as entrees
and i'll still remain hungry and anxious for more
as i gobble up nations and countries

i said i've had an egg on toast
cos that's all there was to eat
yet still i stand upright
and walk on my own feet
so regardless of you thinking you're on top
as you suck from the trough of other men's slops
it's precisely unquenchable gluttony and greed
will bring you and your kind to your knees

silence

in the perfect silence
before the football match
everyone imagining the hell
that burned through paris
a child four rows in front
looks at its father's face
and wonders why his voice
has stopped

in paris
one hundred and thirty
voices have stopped
voices of friends and mothers
sisters
lovers
fathers
brothers
enemies and strangers
acquaintances and neighbours

in the perfect silence
before the football match
the count of stopped voices
does not include those
propagandists of the deed
who dreamed of angels
and halls of paradise
gained through this deliverance
in blood and fire
but found only darkness
and the eternal nothing

millions of voices
have been stopped
by the loud ones who
demand to be heard
over the storm of planes
armoured vehicles
drones
intoning their bitter hymn
about their peace and freedom
and their rule of law

we all stand silent
we all keep quiet
we think the silent other
is the threat

paris 13 november 2015

(Hasna Ait Boulahcen, one of the Paris bombers at the Bataclan Centre, apparently did not blow herself up but was heard fearfully calling for help. One of the other male bombers then detonated her explosive jacket.)

the young woman
who combed her hair every morning
paying attention to the slow tumble
of each strand coming
to rest in the right place
straps herself in
for the evening's activities

when she was small
she liked to play with her toys
and watch american cartoons
dubbed for french tv
later it was the unexpected wetness
that came from the attention of boys
that shifted her centre of gravity

then she learned about the blood
flowing between burnt out houses
bombed schools and ruined hospitals
the numberless lives shattered
children destroyed
possibilities wasted
and in her search for understanding
somebody gave her god
and the certainty of the absolute

so now
she straps herself in
for the evening's activities
and will go from this flat
through darkening streets
to where the lights sparkle
on crowds of people comfortable
that this is the start of the weekend
and the troubles of workaday routine
can be set aside for a while

she will prepare herself with prayers
to the imagined figure
who wants her to do this
and after a moment's indecision
and sudden cry of panic
a helping hand will finish
the evening's activities

do monsters love in dark recesses?

behind the wire fences
in the smoke and ashy rain
where bones are the foundation
for every road and drain
do monsters love in dark recesses
and is life made possible again

do hands that choked and throttled
caress an infant's sleeping face
shining light into the darkness
of hell's soot-blackened place
do lips that spat out murder
through kissing remedy disgrace

underneath the public image
of the politician's sneer
as he counts the paid for votes
from behind a glass of beer
does the hypocrite still manage
to wipe away a tear

over misdeeds he's promoted
and crimes he has allowed
in the name of a mystified people
who though once free and proud
now do what the papers say
in a cowed and willing crowd

do monsters love in dark recesses
beyond the gaze of innocents
or slaver during fetid dreams
of death and blood and pestilence

ribbons and lace

get me ribbons get me lace
get me pretty things
salt and coal and christmas cake
bells and silver rings

i can't take it in this river
freezing fit to drown
got to get away from here
before it drags me down

get me bunting get me flags
get me scrolls and prayer mats
singing bowls and spinning wheels
and those men in hats

i can't take it in this city
pavements black with rain
got to get away from here
before i die again

get me flowers get me garlands
get me soap and lava bread
birds' feet beaks and lonely feathers
for the dressing of the dead

elective mute

his name was freeman
and the girl was only eight
when he ripped her open and raped her
while her mother was on a date
the girl told her brother
and freeman went to jail
but after just one day
he was a free man again
so her brother and the others
took justice in their hands
and beat to death the rapist
who called himself freeman

but marguerite annie johnson
thought she had killed the man
it was her voice that spoke the sentence
and her tongue that cut him down
so deciding words were fatal
and for fear of her deadly voice
she quietly observed the world
from a silent sacrifice
but mrs flowers sent charles dickens
frances harper and edgar allen poe
shakespeare and the other poets
to sing for her voice to grow
later she'd become a prostitute
a pimp and a nightclub dancer

stand at the shoulder of malcolm x
as a revolutionary romancer
and take up her place
at the head of the crowd
marching for what was right
not just what was allowed
and when her voice was soaring
on the wings of all she knew
the raped little girl annie johnson
was the poet maya angelou

fight night

we had a disagreement
about her place or mine
now we have a conflict
and it's internecine

you know how it goes
when your digging up history
how we ever got together
is a murder mystery

she says i don't remember
when we have an anniversary
i try to make her stop
but she shows no mercy

so i remind her of the time
when i caught her with my friend
they were only drinking coffee
but that row won't end

we had a disagreement
about her place or mine
now we have a conflict
and it's internecine

but i don't know how
to make things stop
and she keeps pushing
cos she feels on top

i kick a car
and the alarm goes off
she does a mocking laugh
and i've had enough

i thought i wanted sex
but now i just want silence
before this verbal sparring
turns to physical violence

we had a disagreement
about her place or mine
now we have a conflict
and it's internecine

she wants to make it better
but i won't let it be
unless she's really sorry
and turns into me

i'm cutting off my nose
to spite my face
it always ends like this
in my disgrace

i'm cutting off my nose
to spite my face
it always ends like this
in my disgrace

we had a disagreement
about her place or mine
now we have a conflict
and it's internecine

for lynn

poetry
often as not
creeps up behind the somnolent

as cosy in the certainty of apathy
we while away our time with repetitions
and the comfort of an orange peel

stripped off
in one
continuous
curl

it comes
to stick a bony finger of doubt
deep into the soft tissue
of security

doubt about love and life and death
and pissing yourself in a rainstorm
or at the public baths cos who
would know the difference

and then
when poetry has crept up

it doesn't appear in lines
of times new roman
stumbling across a barren page
or in the mumblings of some old guy
with a chequered past
involving universities and women

but
rather
turns up in a moment

like when the letter you're expecting
falls with a gently awakening flap
on the cold hall floor
just as your stirring mind imagines it

or when the all clear in the cancer war
is sounded one year to the day
a very year to the very day
since the priest read out your name
on all souls

and it's only poetry
poetry creeping up
behind
the somnolent

god's lonely man

it seems i'm going round in circles
one direction's no direction at all
can't see forward back or sideways
don't know if my back's against the wall
so i'm holding myself in readiness
waiting for the prince of heaven's call

and then in one of my more sordid moments
sticky fingers reminding me where i am
on my own with daylight seeping
through the curtains like it doesn't give a damn
i remember how i got to be so solitary
how i became god's lonely man

i thought she wanted me or liked me enough
maybe even entertained respect
and though i was only looking for fun
things didn't go like you'd expect
i sailed right into her whirlpool
and then my ship got wrecked

now i'm a guided fucken missile
fully wound and armed for attack
coming at you in your school or office
gonna knock you on your back

i'm heat-seeking for my targets
and when i find them i won't miss
some people are destined for finer things
but i was meant for this

so i've sorted out my trajectory
and compensated for wind and range
now i'm delivering my retaliation
though getting it in first seems strange
it's the minimum sanction necessary
for achieving the desired change

i'm a guided fucken missile
fully wound and armed for attack
coming at you in your field or factory
i'm gonna knock you on your back

snail

the tiny snail on my shower curtain
has extended itself twice the length
of its round brown shell
and tentacles are taking bearings

i know
or think
i am in the bathroom
but does the snail know where it is
and that it's moving pointlessly
across that white expanse

i choose to imagine that the snail
loves and hates and desires
after it's own fashion
and is moving with a special kind
of snailly insistence
but perhaps it's just another brother
on the outskirts of existence
where all the usual sufferings take place
without any of the imaginings
that put a smile on your face

without my dreams i would be a snail
miserably moving in a bathroom
with no idea where i am
and no hopes
for where i might end up
just another brother
on the outskirts of existence
not your lover
but preoccupied with distance
and though trying to extend
beyond the shell
not doing it so well

journey

she comes
over the brow of memories
through mists
of forgetfulness
and he waits
not knowing who is coming
what she is bringing
how it will be

but under the weathered cloak
of lived experience
a withered child is shivering
with the chill of doubt
unsettled fearfulness
and dread
of the looming other
who is coming

coming from his future
already knowing
his fate
while he imagines
easy happiness
but sees the dreadful
desolation of the heart
and lives in sighs

and so she comes
and he will wait
though tremulous
of what will be his fate
for nothing can be done
to stay the flow
and stem the tide
of what he does not know

remembrance

on a wet back street in a northern town
as the milky sun was going down
a man pulled a gun from inside his coat
and pressed the cold barrel to his soft white throat
but just before he squeezed the trigger and died
he remembered how the chips danced as they fried
in the pitch black cauldrons of berriman's van
and he started to think he'd been a lucky man

he remembered how he stood in the drizzling rain
with pennies in his hand to pay for chips again
inhaling the aroma of warm vinegar and salt
and he thought to bring his suicide to a halt
but there's something about metal when it's pressed against skin
that reminded him that life's a game you cannot win
so he squeezed a little more almost to a click
and knew if he was going he'd better be off quick

then in his other hand he felt the warming paper
and remembered how he sometimes used to read the news
in the northern echo wrapped around his supper
as he tried to make sense of the crossword clues
and he saw the boy smiling as he ate his fill
reading spennymoor two blyth spartans nil
and he'd almost imagined life used to be fun
when he squeezed a little more and remembrance was done

screwball ruffian

she liked him cos he was a screwball ruffian
no airs and graces didn't give a damn
but underneath there was a trembling soul
who'd been born dropped and was a falling man

so when she got in close and opened him
and looking saw the fear inside
she held him like a flower to sooth his pain
and swore that she would never leave his side

but he wouldn't believe her he couldn't take the chance
of trusting the steps of the lovers' dance
so instead he set her tests and laid his traps
till eventually he proved she was a liar

but she hadn't lied it's just he wore her down
set her up to be an angel wearing heaven's crown
then proved she was a woman who could suffer too
when he burned her in his jealous fire

she liked him cos he was screwball ruffian
but behind that knelt a lost and lonely child
who never trusted smiles or a guiding hand
and covered by pretending to be wild

she liked him cos he was a screwball ruffian
but he wasn't any ruffian at all
and when at last he'd broken her and made her leave
no one was there to see him take the fall
when he put that chair behind the door
cos he didn't want to be here anymore
and he couldn't work out what he was for
though he thought he heard the final score

coming through the sound of his scrambling feet
like the echoing words of his own deceit
as he visited the cold slap of defeat
on the one true face he'd ever meet

she liked him cos he was a screwball ruffian
no airs and graces didn't seem to give a damn
but underneath there was an crippled soul
who'd been born dropped and was a broken man

home time

eight years old walking home from school
splashing patent leather in a muddy pool
saw a nest in the hedge with a couple of eggs
felt the cold water running down her legs

then when she got home, saw a message on the door
'don't come in there's no one here anymore
'you'd better go straight round to your gran's
'just go there and wait for your mam'

but she couldn't resist couldn't hold herself back
so she tried the letterbox and lifted the flap
little fingers held it open as she looked in
and what she saw she knew was him

it was her daddy's feet dangling by the staircase
it was her daddy's shoes floating in the air
it was her daddy's feet dangling by the staircase
it was her daddy's shoes floating in the air

so she went to her granny's till her mother came home
when she heard her talking on the telephone
then the ambulance came and the policemen too
but nobody told her what she had to do

except 'look at your legs and those filthy shoes
'sometimes it's like you haven't got a clue'
when granny put her to bed, she couldn't go to sleep
cos something kept appearing from the blackest deep

it was her daddy's feet dangling by the staircase
it was her daddy's shoes floating in the air
it was her daddy's feet dangling by the staircase
it was her daddy's shoes floating in the air

and for the rest of her life she's going to have that picture
for the rest of her life she's going live that scene
for the rest of her life this little girl will wonder
if what she saw was really what she'd seen

it was her daddy's feet dangling by the staircase
it was her daddy's shoes floating in the air
it was her daddy's feet dangling by the staircase
it was her daddy's shoes floating in the air

the news

they found a desiccated baby at the back of the fire
and when they interviewed the mother she was clearly a liar
the circumstances were enough to make you go mad
and the baby never even had a sight of its dad

it's not just an aspect of the modern world
it's how things have been since the start of time
getting rid of inconvenience is de rigueur
some don't even think the killing is a crime

well blow me down and knock me senseless
the way things are going i'll soon be defenceless
i do my best to keep a handle on things
but i lose it the minute eliza carthy sings

they're blowing up the tunnels that medicine comes through
and putting up a fence to keep me away from you
grabbing up the land like they're rolling up a carpet
then programming the drones to select their target

someone's in the kitchen sorting through his guns
then heading to the high school to have some fun
before the day is over there'll be plenty dead
and somewhere a journalist will lose his head

well blow me down and knock me senseless
the way things are going i'll soon be defenceless
i do my best to keep a handle on things
but i lose it the minute eliza carthy sings

homecoming

the fire was burning low
and i was sitting by the radio
listening to the record show
when my girl came home

she came through the door quietly
lay her coat on the red settee
said something about it not being me
when my girl came home

i asked her what it was she'd said
she shrugged and dropped her head
i thought she'd heard someone was dead
when my girl came home

hank williams was singing cheating heart
and i thought this was poetry at work
when she started to cry and apologise
and said she knew that i'd be hurt

but things just happen to people like us
you can't see what's coming your way
and she'd never imagined saying these words
never wanted to come to this day

then she took a deep breath
from behind her tears
and told me that the baby was gone
i didn't know she was pregnant
couldn't start to feel the loss

when my girl came home
when my girl came home

the river wear

i'd rather be in durham in the pouring rain
than anywhere on earth and not see her again
the gentle bending of her slender knee
beneath the redbronzegolden autumn leaves
closes between her calf and thigh
a longing hand that's reaching for the sky

here the river turns
and in a moment of geometry
becomes a bastion
surrounding sacred dreams
this is her sacrifice
to turn and bend revisiting herself
in passing by her spreading form

she always knew that
though straight lines may get you
where you want to go more quickly
and with less trouble on the whole
love and history do not follow easy paths
but call for those contortions of the heart and soul
that make a river bend
a mountain grow
a cathedral to appear from the human hand

so she forsook the shorter path
and gave herself to rocks and tumbling weirs
creating the safe almost-island
where lives and loves and dreams
could be fulfilled in stone and shining glass
blessed by her waters for ten hundred years
on every quiet pass

and though a thousand years went by
without an answer to our aching cries
she stayed and wound herself around
the miracle that we drew from the ground
so i will be in durham in the pouring rain
rather than never be with her again

mother

when autumn chimneys whispered smokey promises to clouds
and crows like sooty kisses greeted trees
my mother pushed the sturdy pram
on cushioned walks of sodden leaves
and conkers ready for the string

at home the baby had its cosy cot
and i was laid to snuggle on the couch
but she could claim the kitchen's concrete floor
cold cure for the curse i couldn't comprehend
and lay there with a wincing promise to survive

and so survive is what she did
through all my turbulence and storms
the riot contradiction of my wild becoming
the broken hearts spilt dreams dropped hopes
and resurrection after every fall

she stayed with me and held my hand
when i would slap and push away
declare my hate for everything i loved
and my despising of the ones
i really most admired

until that day in january eighty-two
when darkness fell upon her like a shadow hand
and women weeping rang the hollow bell
to tell a heedless world that it was done
and home was turned from nest to blackened bough
i sat beside her on the bed where earlier
each touch was pain no kitchen floor could quell
i combed her hair i stroked her brow i wished her stay
but she was gone and i was left to say
goodbye not once but ever and a day

when you are lonely

when you are lonely and the birds have gone
binoculars won't bring them back
though for a while they may seem closer
truth is the past has flown

each day you'll search for evidence of them
in sounds that may be singing
or the fading beating of a little wing

but though you see the moving speck
imagining it's closing in
departed dreams do not return
not even with the blossoming of spring

so every day you dream anew
imagining the past is in the now
but your present is the past that flew

what matters now below the clouded sky
is looking straight at what you see
taking in hand the fact of how things are
and living with the loss make yourself free

stars

i am in the dark red depthless troublestash
of cordwainers and revenue men and tinker boys and sailors
of anarchists with frosty eyes and underground tailors
of bolsheviks and mensheviks and preoccupied whalers
of therapists who treat the healthy
taxmen who rebate the wealthy
runners who ignore the stealthy
and stargazers who count no stars

i am in the place of dumbfounds
who never speak for fear of conjured storms
but kneel counting contraband on a camomile lawn
and gather morsels of thought dribbled just before dawn
by the weary and cold who would like to be warm
by the right and the wrong
by the many and the one
by the old wordless song of the stars

so i creep in the darkness
without any bright sense
of the spin of the bittersweet compass
and console all my fearful children and pets
with the promise of superabundance
cold fusion and thorium and driverless cars
and think that the future and also the past
takes place amongst numberless stars

Thirteen Points For The 'Not A Poet' Manifesto

1.

Whoever fears flying is not a Poet.

2.

Those who believe flying involves aeroplanes, rocket ships, hot air balloons, gliders or kites are not Poets.

3.

Anyone adhering to conventions of form and language, instead of subverting them, is not a Poet.

4.

He who sees the knife but does not recognise the radiance of the blade is not a Poet.

5.

People who need alcohol or drugs to become intoxicated, or avoid alcohol and drugs for fear of intoxication, are not Poets.

6.

Whoever imagines the pen is mightier than the sword is not a Poet.

7.

Someone for whom thought and emotion are less real than flesh, and the flesh not confirmation of thought and emotion, is not a Poet.

8.

A person who believes one and one only make two is not a Poet.

9.

A man who thinks the exploration of outer space or the ocean's depth is more important than the exploration of the back of a woman's knee is not a Poet.

10.

If you think poetry is a more honest way of making money than being a teacher, an engineer, a doctor, a cleaner, a road sweeper or an undertaker you are not a Poet.

11.

To comply with the demands of reality is to not be a Poet.

12.

Anyone who thinks the word 'cunt' refers to part of a woman's body rather than the transformative state in which she becomes capable of flight (see points 1 and 2) is not a Poet.

13.

Whoever agrees with three or more of these points should establish a new movement of Poetry.

photography

Marc A Price takes photographs. Often in black and white. His work has been used on the covers of books and CDs and has been described as dark and sinister. He is still convinced that all he does is point the camera in the right direction and shoots what he sees.

Marc was born in Peterborough, Cambridgeshire in the UK but reached escape velocity in his late teens and has moved around a lot since. He currently lives in the Netherlands with his wife and two children.

The images for *Hot strawberries* are further expressions of the subject matter. Sometimes they express the space between the lines of the poetry and sometimes just show what is on the page.

Aimee Reid is a talented actor and dramatist, who also performs as a solo singer/guitarist.

She features on the ReidGraves album, *Lovely As Suspicion*, providing backing vocals on one track and beautifully taking the lead on another, *Arithmetic*.

She is also a capable photographer who provided pictures for that album and the back cover of this book.

ALSO FROM LEB BOOKS

Gillian Large began life the hard way in the West Midlands in the late 1940s.

Although her mother had a wealthy, privileged upbringing, Gillian was born into an inner world of squalor and chaos.

In *It's Always the Children*, Gillian takes you on a roller coaster ride of her early family life in the 50s and 60s to womanhood with courage, inner strength and humour.

"A very honest account of shocking emotional and physical abuse"

⭐⭐⭐⭐⭐

ISBN 978-0957314177
£11.99

Bill Cawley has been described as "a continual seeker after facts".

This collection of over 80 original articles will entertain and amaze you in equal measure.

Bill's knowledge of the Staffordshire Moorlands - its people, its culture and its history - is encyclopaedic. *Tales From The Hills* takes you on a journey into the past culled from the archives of

"something for everyone"

⭐⭐⭐⭐⭐

ISBN 978-0957314191
£11.99

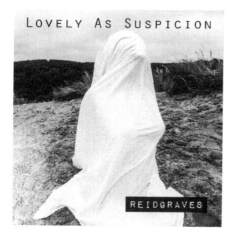

LOVELY AS SUSPICION

The central theme of the album, *Lovely As Suspicion*, is that both joy and misery inevitably arise from living. There is death, broken heartedness, betrayal, abuse and frustrated hope. There is also tenderness, compassion, humour and the joy of being absolutely in love. The album closes with a straight middle finger held up to the world. *Lovely As Suspicion* is their first CD.

Label: Secret Shark via CDbaby (888295373579) on CD and Digital
Released: 15th January 2016

Available from www.reidgraves.com
Amazon, CD Baby, Google Play, Spotify, Deezer, All Music, and just about anywhere else you want to try, as a CD or digital download.

Overend Watts (founder member and bass guitar, Mott the Hoople):
'I have to say it is a really STUNNING piece of work and sort of breaks new ground. It is also very moreish – I MUST play it over & over – I have NO choice!'

Tim Jones (Stone Premonitions Records):
'I think that the album is excellent and the lyrics very challenging and thought provoking. The guitar playing reminded me of Richard Thompson at times. This is a superb piece of work. I love the artwork too – intriguing!'

Peter Anderson (Raiders FM):
'(*Ain't Blues*) is an outstanding track ... a gem of an album'

Lord Litter
(International DJ and a leading figure of the alternative music scene):
'...a brilliant, unique piece of underground culture'

Barry 'DJ Bazza' Mart (TBRM Radio):
'There is some really good stuff on this album, I've been playing tracks (*Ain't Blues*, and *Sign Up*) on the show and they went down really well.'

Printed in Great Britain
by Amazon